GEO DETECTIVES
THE WATER CYCLE

Anita Ganeri & Chris Oxlade

Illustrated by **Pau Morgan**

Curriculum consultant **Richard Hatwood**

QEB

Hello, I'm Ava
and this is George.
We're the Geo Detectives!

Our job is to discover all
about natural wonders
on Earth. Come with us
as we explore!

Quarto is the authority on a wide range of topics.

Quarto educates, entertains and enriches the lives of
our readers—enthusiasts and lovers of hands-on living.

www.quartoknows.com

Author: Anita Ganeri and Chris Oxlade
Illustrator: Pau Morgan
Consultant: Michael Bright
Curriculum consultant: Richard Hatwood
Editor: Harriet Stone
Designer: Sarah Chapman-Suire
Editorial Director: Laura Knowles

© 2019 Quarto Publishing plc
This edition first published in 2019
by QEB Publishing,
an imprint of The Quarto Group.
6 Orchard Road, Suite 100
Lake Forest, CA 92630
T: +1 949 380 7510
F: +1 949 380 7575
www.QuartoKnows.com

A CIP record for this book is available from the
Library of Congress.

ISBN 978 0 7112 4464 1

Manufactured in Guangdong, China TT072019

9 8 7 6 5 4 3 2 1

Picture Credits
(t=top, b=bottom, l=left, r=right, fc=front cover)

Shutterstock
7 Denis Burdin, 9 Maxim Petrichuk, 13 Mny-Jhee,
fc and 15 Tatahnka, 19 Barbara Rogers, fc and
21 Oleksandr Mazur, 23 Sergey Lyashenko, 25
mikeshinmaksim,

Alamy
27 Richard Ellis, 28 Angelo Hornak

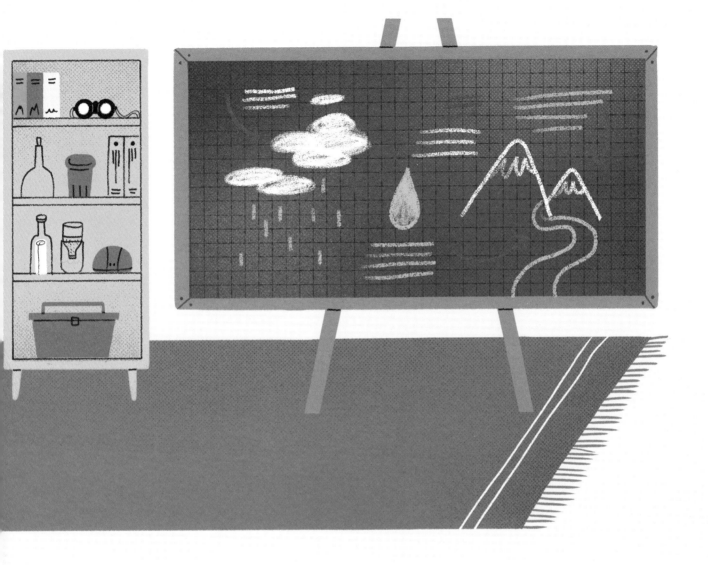

Contents

The wonderful water cycle

Join Ava and George as they investigate the Earth's water cycle. They'll be using their detective skills as they travel around in the clouds, fall to the ground with the raindrops, and get swept along rivers, in the amazing water cycle. You can help by trying out the activities for yourself.

The Geo Detectives are ready to go!

Rainwater is pouring down from the clouds in the sky. It trickles across the ground, into a river, and then into the sea.

We're going to investigate on the ground and up in the sky, to learn about the water cycle.

Look at these fluffy clouds! They are part of the water cycle. Let's find out how clouds are formed.

Water is always on the move around the water cycle. It travels from the sea into the air, from the air to the ground, and from the ground into streams and rivers that carry it back to the sea. Then around it goes again!

GEO FACT

Without the water cycle, all the land on Earth would be a giant **desert!**

The world's water

Deep oceans of water cover about two-thirds of the Earth's surface. There's also water in lakes, rivers, under the ground, in the air, and at the icy poles. Join the Geo Detectives to learn about the different types of water on Earth.

There are two types of water in the water cycle. The water in the seas and oceans is **saltwater**. The water in clouds, rain, and rivers is **freshwater**. Freshwater doesn't have any salt in it.

Yuk! This water tastes salty. It's full of minerals, like salt that you put on your food.

The water in this river is fresh. It's on its way to the sea. The water we drink is always freshwater rather than saltwater.

Never drink water straight from a river or the sea, as it might have nasty germs in it!

GEO FACT

Some of the thick ice in Antarctica is made from snow that fell millions of years ago!

Finding Earth's water

What you need:
• tablet or computer

Google Earth is like a globe on your tablet or computer screen. Use it to see all the water on planet Earth.

1. Ask an adult to install and start the Google Earth application for you.

2. Zoom out so you can see the whole planet.

3. Spin the Earth until you can see the Pacific Ocean—between America and Australia. Can you find the Atlantic Ocean and the Indian Ocean too?

4. Look for the continent of Antarctica. It is covered in frozen water.

5. Use Google Earth's search box to find Lake Baikal. This huge lake contains one fifth of the world's freshwater.

6. Now search for the Amazon River. Rain that falls in the Amazon rainforest flows down the Amazon River to the sea. Can you follow the river all the way to the Atlantic Ocean?

Most of the world's water is in the oceans. The giant Pacific Ocean covers nearly half of the Earth. The deepest part of the Pacific is nearly 7 miles (11 km) deep. That's taller than Mount Everest!

Lots of the world's freshwater is frozen. It's in **glaciers**, in thick icebergs at the Earth's **poles**, and on snowy mountains.

7

Liquid, solid, or gas

Water can be a **liquid**, a solid, or a **gas**. The Geo Detectives are in a rainforest finding out about the gas form of water, called **water vapor**.

The air in a rainforest contains lots of water vapor. Liquid water from the damp ground and the dripping wet undergrowth turns to gas because it's so hot here. This change is called **evaporation**.

What you need:
• sock
• glass jar
• ice cubes
• window
• water

GEO FACT

When it cools down, water vapor in the air turns back to liquid water. This change is called **condensation**.

Looking for water vapor

Water vapor is all around us. Evaporation and condensation are going on all the time. Let's go and find them!

1. Fill a jar with ice cubes. Add some cold water and swirl it around. Watch the outside of the jar. Can you see tiny droplets of water?

The ice makes the jar very cold. The air around the jar also cools down, so water vapor in the air turns to liquid water. This is condensation.

2. Put a sock into cold water. Squeeze out as much water as you can. Hang the sock somewhere sunny and check it every half an hour. Slowly the cloth will feel drier. Where do you think the water is going?

Heat from the Sun turns the water in the sock into water vapor. This is evaporation.

3. Breathe out slowly onto a cool window or mirror. What appears on the glass?

Tiny water droplets form on the glass. The water is part of the air you breathe out. This is condensation.

Weird! I can see liquid water, but water vapor in the air is invisible.

When there's lots of water vapor in the air, it feels sticky and **humid**. It's hard for the sweat on your skin to dry up.

Water is made up of tiny bits called **molecules.** In water vapor the molecules are more spread out than they are in liquid water or ice.

Use your detective skills to find other examples of water vapor.

Ice is the solid form of water. It is made when liquid water gets so cold that it freezes. Ice turns back to liquid water when it warms up.

Going around and around

The water cycle is a nonstop journey. Ava and George will follow it from the sea to high up in the air, down to the land, and then back to the sea again.

1. The Sun heats the sea. Water evaporates from the surface of the sea and turns to water vapor.

Phew it's hot today! The hotter it is, the faster the water evaporates.

GEO FACT

Water spends about ten days in the **atmosphere** before it falls back to the ground.

2. Up in the air the water vapor cools down and makes clouds in the sky.

3. Water falls to the ground as rain, snow, or **hail**.

So the rain falling on my head came all the way from the sea! Wow!

4. The water flows along streams and rivers back to the sea.

What you need:
- plastic wrap
- ice cubes
- cup
- warm water
- bowl

Water cycle model

Make a simple model of the water cycle.

1. Pour warm water into the bowl until it is about about 1 inch (2.5 cm) deep.

2. Stand the cup in the bowl.

3. Cover the bowl with plastic wrap.

4. Put a few ice cubes in the center of the film, above the cup.

5. Watch what happens inside the bowl. It will take a few minutes to see the results.

Water evaporates from the bowl as water vapor. The water vapor cools and condenses when it gets close to the ice. The liquid water then drips back into the cup, just like rain falling in the water cycle.

Into the sky

Next the Geo Detectives are going to look at each step of the water cycle close-up. Their journey starts out at sea. This is where seawater evaporates into the atmosphere.

When the Sun shines on the sea, the water on the sea's surface warms up. The warm water evaporates into water vapor which goes into the air. The warm air carrying the water vapor starts to rise.

I wonder what happens to the salt when seawater evaporates?

Nothing! It stays in the sea. Only the water evaporates, leaving the salt behind.

GEO FACT

Plants are part of the water cycle too. They take up water from the soil and give out water vapor into the air. This is called transpiration.

Evaporation from the sea

Let's see how heat from the Sun makes water evaporate from the oceans and rise into the atmosphere.

What you need:
- two identical bowls
- water
- food coloring
- ruler

1. Half fill each bowl with water and add a few drops of food coloring. Measure how deep the water is in each bowl and write it down.

2. Put one bowl on a sunny windowsill and one bowl in a shady place indoors.

3. Every two hours look at the bowls and measure how deep the water is. Which bowl lost its water more quickly?

Remember, hotter weather makes water evaporate faster. So more water vapor rises into the air in hot parts of the world.

The bowl in the sunny spot loses water more quickly. The warm Sun makes water evaporate more quickly, just like in the water cycle.

Water evaporates from the land as well as the sea, from damp soil and puddles.

Making clouds

Now Ava and George are high up in the atmosphere among the clouds! Water vapor that came from the sea turns to water or ice in the atmosphere. This makes the clouds we see in the sky.

When you breathe out on a cold day, water vapor in your breath turns into tiny water droplets that you can see, just like a cloud.

Warm air containing water vapor rises up into the atmosphere. As it rises, it cools down. This makes the water vapor condense—turning from a gas to a liquid. Sometimes it's so cold that the water vapor turns to ice. Water and ice both sit in the atmosphere as clouds.

Look at these clouds forming! On a warm day, you can see the air swirling around and watch clouds growing.

GEO FACT

Clouds look white or gray because the drops or crystals reflect light from the Sun.

If you could look closely inside a cloud you would see billions of tiny water droplets or ice crystals.

Sometimes the wind blows air up over mountains. As the air rises up it cools down, so clouds often form over mountains.

What you need:
• large jar with lid
• hot water
• ice cubes
• hairspray

Cloud in a jar

Here's how to make your very own mini cloud inside a jar.

1. Ask an adult to pour about 1 inch (2.5 cm) of hot water into the jar.

2. Fill the jar lid with some ice cubes.

3. Squirt a small amount of hairspray into the jar.

4. Place the lid on the jar the wrong way up, so the ice sits on top.

5. Watch carefully inside the jar. Do you see a cloud?

The warm water evaporates, filling the jar with water vapor. The ice makes the water vapor cool, forming tiny water droplets. The tiny particles of hairspray help the water droplets to form, which makes the cloud thicker.

All sorts of clouds

Up in the sky the Geo Detectives are investigating clouds of many shapes and sizes—clumpy ones, fluffy ones, flat ones, and wispy ones. They are all made from water droplets or ice crystals.

Each type of cloud has a different name. You can see some of them here.

Cumulonimbus

Cirrocumulus

GEO FACT

A giant cumulonimbus cloud can contain one million tons of water!

What you need:
• guide to different clouds, such as the one on this page
• paper
• pencil

Cloud watching

1. Go outdoors and look up into the sky. Can you see any of the clouds in your cloud guide?

2. Make a simple sketch of the clouds you can see.

3. Write down the date and time, and what the weather is like.

4. On a warm day when lots of fluffy clouds are forming, watch the tops of the clouds carefully. Can you see the clouds changing shape and growing as more and more water droplets form inside them?

These wispy clouds high up in the sky are also known as mare's tails because they look like the tails of horses.

Some clouds are very high up in the sky. The highest are more than 7.5 miles (12 km) up.

Cirrus

Look! These clouds are in heaps. That's what the word cumulus means. Some clouds are in layers. That's what the word stratus means.

Altocumulus

Stratocumulus

Cumulus

Stratus

Some clouds are low in the sky, near to the ground. The tops of tall hills are sometimes hidden in low clouds.

Back to Earth

In the next step of the water cycle, water in clouds falls back to the ground. The Geo Detectives are traveling with it. Any water that falls from the sky, such as rain, snow, or hail, is called precipitation.

Big raindrops fall faster than small raindrops. How big do you think a raindrop can get?

As more and more water vapor turns to liquid water inside clouds, the droplets or ice crystals get larger and larger. This makes clouds thicker.

When you walk through low, misty clouds, you can see the tiny droplets of water swirling around.

GEO FACT

The biggest raindrops ever seen were 1/3 inch (9 mm) across. That's about the same size as a marble!

When the water droplets get big enough, they fall towards the ground as rain. Ice crystals often melt as they fall through the air, but if it's very cold they fall to the ground as snow.

What you need:
- 2-liter plastic bottle
- small stones
- plastic ruler
- scissors
- waterproof tape
- paper and pen

Hailstones fall from big cumulonimbus clouds. They are a made when frozen raindrops go around and around in the cloud collecting into a ball.

Catching rainfall

Scientists measure how much rain has fallen using a rain gauge. It catches falling rain and stores it ready to be measured.

1. Ask an adult to help you cut around the bottle, about two-thirds of the way up, to give you two parts.

2. Put a few small stones in the bottom of the bottle. They will stop it from falling over in the wind.

3. Remove the bottle top, turn the top section over, and slide it into the bottom section. Fix in place with waterproof tape.

4. Tape the ruler to the bottle so that the zero mark is above the small stones and the curve at the bottle's base.

5. Pour water into the bottle until it is level with the zero mark on the ruler. Now your rain gauge is ready to use.

6. Put the rain gauge outside, away from buildings and trees.

7. Read the rain gauge at the same time each day. Write down the day and the amount of rainfall in millimeters.

8. After taking a reading, empty out the water until it is back to zero on the ruler.

Into the sea

Ava and George have reached the end of their journey around the water cycle. This is where water flows from the land along rivers and into the sea. It gets back to where it started at the beginning of the cycle.

Some of the rain that lands on the ground trickles downhill. It finds its way into streams. This is called runoff.

When it rains hard, look out for water running downhill. It will flow into your local river.

What you need:
• plastic tray
• sand
• watering can with water
• piece of wood or a brick

Water shapes the land

Make a simple model to see how river water washes rock from one place to another. Do this activity outdoors.

1. Fill the tray with sand about 1 inch (2.5 cm) deep.

2. Prop one end of the tray up on a block of wood or a brick.

3. Sprinkle water from the watering can onto the sand near the top of the tray and watch what happens to the sand.

The water from the watering can works like rain falling on the land. It gathers into little streams as it runs down the tray. It carries sand with it, just as a river carries tiny bits of rock from the land to the sea.

When mountain snow melts in spring, the water flows into rivers. The water in the snow has been trapped all winter but now returns to the water cycle.

GEO FACT

The Amazon River dumps enough water into the Atlantic Ocean to fill 50 Olympic swimming pools every second!

Remember that the water in rivers is freshwater. It mixes with salty seawater when it flows into the sea.

Streams join together to make bigger streams and these join together to make rivers. The rivers flow across the land to the sea.

Underground water

Some of the rain that lands on the ground soaks into the soil. This water is called groundwater. Let's go underground with Ava and George to see where the water goes.

Some water flows into caves and through underground passageways. When there's not much rain, the water trickles through slowly, but when it pours, the caves can fill up.

Did you know that trickling water wears away rock? Very slowly it makes the caves bigger and the passages wider.

GEO FACT

When soil is completely soaked with water, the water often seeps out of the ground. The place where the water comes out is called a **spring**.

What you need:

- plastic bottle
- sand
- gravel
- scrap of cotton cloth
- soil from the garden
- jug

Rocky filters

Water gets cleaned as it trickles down through layers of rock. Underground water is normally very clean. Let's see how this happens.

1. Ask an adult to help you cut off the bottom third of the bottle.

2. Take off the lid and put the top section of the bottle upside down into the other section.

3. Push a scrap of cotton tightly into the neck of the bottle.

4. Make a 2-inch (5 cm) layer of sand on top of the cotton.

5. Make a 2-inch (5 cm) layer of gravel on top of the sand.

6. Add some soil to a jug of water and slowly pour it into the top of your filter.

7. Wait for the water to trickle into the base of the bottle.

Did your filter clean the muddy water? Don't drink your filtered water, as it might still have germs in it.

It's funny to see a stream coming out from underground!

At the end of a cave, an underground stream flows back outside. The water joins other streams and rivers on the way back to the sea.

The useful water cycle

Freshwater is a very important natural resource. We need it for drinking, washing, and growing crops. Follow the Geo Detectives to find out where we get freshwater from.

We store freshwater in large lakes called **reservoirs**. A thick wall called a **dam** traps water from streams and rivers, making a reservoir.

Wide pipes let water out of the reservoirs so that it doesn't overflow.

This reservoir looks a bit empty! It will fill up again when there's lots of rain and more water comes down the river.

GEO FACT

Sometimes people get their water from under the ground. A well reaches down to the water that is deep below the surface.

A water wheel

What you need:
• two unwanted CDs or DVDs
• six plastic bottle tops
• wooden spoon
• hot-glue gun

1. Put one of the CDs down flat.

2. Ask an adult to glue the edges of six bottle tops to the CD, so they are all facing counterclockwise.

3. Add glue to the top edges of all the bottle tops and put the other CD on top, making sure it lines up with the bottom CD.

4. Slide a wooden spoon handle through the holes in the CDs.

5. Hold the wheel under a gently running tap so that the water catches in the lids. Watch the wheel spin!

We can use running water to turn a wheel and create electricty.

There's a hole like a giant plughole down here! This is where the water must go when the reservoir gets too full.

In some places, we capture the energy in flowing water and turn it into electricity.

Looking after water

The Geo Detectives are investigating how humans make water dirty. If we want clean water to drink, and to give to animals and plants, we need to start looking after it better.

Yuk! This water is too dirty for anyone to drink.

Some factories pour nasty chemicals into streams and rivers. And sometimes, dirty sewage water goes into rivers.

People throw trash into rivers. Rivers get clogged up with plastic bags and bottles. The plastic also gets carried into oceans. Ava and George are litter-picking to help clean up this river.

GEO FACT

Global warming is changing the water cycle. Some places are getting drier and some are getting wetter.

Make a difference!

You can help to reduce water pollution and stop wasting water by following the three Rs—Reduce, Reuse, and Recycle. Here are some ideas:

1. Reduce your plastic and water use:
   - Never use plastic straws or plastic cutlery
   - Don't leave taps running while you brush your teeth
   - Spend less time in the shower.

2. Reuse plastic and water:
   - Refill plastic bottles with water instead of buying new bottles
   - Reuse shopping bags instead of buying new ones.

3. Recycle plastics:
   - Always put plastic in the recycling. Look for the recycling symbol on plastic bottles and containers.

The trash that gets into rivers and the sea can harm animals that live there.

Marine animals such as turtles are harmed by plastic waste that's washed into the oceans.

Geo Detective quiz

Now help Ava and George answer these Geo Detective questions. How much did you learn as you explored the water cycle?

1. What's the difference between seawater and freshwater?

2. What is the gas form of water called?

3. What happens to water when it evaporates?

4. What happens to water vapor when it cools down?

5. What are clouds made of?

6. What are fluffy, heaped clouds called?

7. What's the name for layered clouds?

8. What is the name of this huge cloud that brings thunderstorms?

9. Can you list three different types of precipitation?

10. What do we use to measure rainfall?

11. What's the name for water that runs off the land and into rivers?

12. Where might you find groundwater?

13. What's the name of a lake that stores drinking water?

14. What material that we throw away is clogging up our rivers and the oceans?

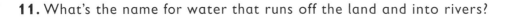

ANSWERS

1. Seawater tastes salty because it had salt dissolved in it. Freshwater doesn't contain salt.
2. Water vapor. 3. It turns into water vapor. 4. It turns back to liquid water in a process called condensation. 5. Tiny drops of water or ice crystals. 6. Cumulus clouds. 7. Stratus clouds.
8. Cumulonimbus cloud. 9. Rain, snow, and hail. 10. A rain gauge. 11. Runoff. 12. Under the ground.
13. A reservoir. 14. Plastic objects, such as plastic bags and bottles

Glossary

atmosphere layer of air that surrounds the Earth

condensation when a gas, such as water vapor, turns into a liquid, such as water

dam strong, thick wall or bank that holds back the water in a reservoir

desert very dry area of land with few plants

evaporation when a liquid turns into a gas, such as water turning into water vapor

freshwater water that does not contain any salt

gas form of matter, such as air, that expands to fill the container it is in

glacier slow-moving river of ice that moves down from a high mountain

global warming gradual warming of the Earth's atmosphere caused by human activities

hail lumps of ice that fall from a cloud

humid describes air that contains lots of water vapor

liquid form of matter, such as water, that can flow and change shape according to the containers it is in

molecules extremely tiny particles of matter that many substances, including water, are made from

poles two places on the Earth's surface (the North Pole and the South Pole) that are very cold and are in line with the Earth's axis

reservoir human-made lake made by building a dam across a valley to trap water

saltwater water that contains salts and tastes salty, such as seawater

spring place where water trickles out from underground

water vapor gas form of water that is nearly always found in air

Authors' note

Hello,

We hope you have enjoyed reading with the Geo Detectives! Did you learn lots about the water cycle and how it works? Did you try out all the experiments?

We have written many books about lots of different topics, from monster trucks to the solar system, but the Earth we live on is always one of our favorite things to write about. We enjoy being outdoors, kayaking, windsurfing, and sailing. We are often very close to the water, sometimes on lakes, sometimes on flowing rivers, and sometimes in the sea. So we get plenty of chances to see the water cycle in action! We also enjoy climbing mountains, where there always seem to be plenty of clouds and rain!

We live in Yorkshire in England, in a house called Springdale. It's called Springdale because there's a spring in the garden where underground water comes out the ground on it's way around the water cycle.

Chris Oxlade & Anita Ganeri

Find out more

Visit these websites to find out more about the water cycle.

www.metoffice.gov.uk/weather/learn-about/weather/weather-for-kids
Lots of information about the water cycle, clouds, and the weather from the UK Meteorological Office

www.bbc.com/bitesize/articles/z3wpp39
Fun information about the water cycle from the BBC

water.usgs.gov/edu/watercycle-kids-beg.html
An interactive diagram of the water cycle from the United States Geological Survey

pmm.nasa.gov/education/videos/water-cycle-animation
An animated water cycle from NASA

Notes for teachers & parents

Take it further with these extra activities and discussion points for in the classroom, or at home.

In 2014, a record amount of precipitation fell on New York, nearly 60 days' worth of rainfall in just a few hours. How do the children think this might have effected the city? Research the aftereffects and discuss them with the children.

NASA has found that glaciers in East Antarctica are melting very quickly. If the glaciers on Antarctica melt, what do the children think could happen to our planet?

The River Thames flows through the city of London. Sometimes the water level of the Thames gets dangerously high, because it has rained so much. Find out what people are doing to protect London from flooding.

The water cycle has both positive and negative impacts on people. Rising warm air over an ocean can create a hurricane. How do people keep safe during a hurricane? What do the children think experiencing a hurricane would be like?

Lakes contain freshwater, whereas oceans and seas contain saltwater. Use a map to find the largest lake in the US. How do the children think this fits into the water cycle?

Fresh water travels for miles and miles from the source of a river all the way to the river mouth, where it flows into the sea. Some fish swim upstream at certain times of year to lay eggs. What can the children find out about these fish and their upstream journey?

In areas close to rivers or coasts, humans use the power of water to create electricity. What can the children find out about hydropower? How is it better than other types of power?

Index